CALM THOUGHTS

ON THE

RECENT MINUTES OF THE COMMITTEE OF COUNCIL ON EDUCATION,

AND ON THEIR SUPPOSED BEARING UPON

THE INTERESTS OF CIVIL FREEDOM

PROTESTANT NONCONFORMITY.

By HENRY DUNN.

LONDON:

HOULSTON AND STONEMAN,
PATERNOSTER ROW.

Price One Shilling.

CALM THOUGHTS,

&c. &c.

TO A FRIEND.

I SHOULD long ago have stated frankly and fully the
views I entertain in relation to the recent measures of
the Government on Education, had I not been restrained
from so doing, partly by a desire to avoid even the appear-
ance of *committing* the Society with which I am connected,
by the expression of personal opinions; and partly by a
strong, and very natural unwillingness to place myself in
opposition to many of my oldest and warmest friends.

Both these reasons have now ceased to operate. The
explanations recently given to the public, as to the true
position of the Society, by a Member of the Committee,
when presiding over a Meeting called for the purpose of
opposing the " Minutes," will as effectually guard me as
himself from any suspicion of wishing to violate the freedom of the Institution: while the prevalence, in some
quarters, of an impression that I am not acting candidly
in concealing my opinions, more than counterbalances the
regret which I cannot but feel, in being compelled to differ
from many with whom I have hitherto been cordially united.

It is well known that I have never held the doctrine, recently proclaimed with so much vehemence, that it is altogether beyond the province of the Civil Government to promote the instruction of the people. On the contrary, I have always maintained that the State might advantageously *assist*, both in the support of existing schools, and in the establishment of new ones in destitute districts. I still think so. "To say that a government may consistently do its best to help a nation to grow rich, but that it must not be supposed to care a jot about the influence which this money-getting may have upon its habits of industry, its intelligence, or its tone of moral feeling, would be to make distinctions the weakness of which becomes manifest the moment they are stated. Government is the expedient of society, the instrument which society forms for itself, that it may thereby realize its proper end. Society is the master, government is the servant. Man was not made for government, but government was made for man. The question, accordingly, about the province of government resolves itself into a question about the best division of labour. Hence, if it can be made to appear, that popular education, like provision for the poor, would be best conducted by admitting a certain measure of agency from the government, it would be legitimate to admit that agency. That children should obey their parents is a principle, and that subjects should obey their sovereign is a principle; but there is a still higher principle having respect to the highest parentage and the highest sovereignty, to which the other principles named are subordinate. In like manner, it may be the duty of a government to become an educator to a certain extent, and there may be a wider view of the general interest, requiring that it should not become an educator beyond a certain point. In no respect are men betrayed into error on questions of this nature more commonly, than in their attempts to lay down immutable rules, to be applicable in their fullest extent, to all circumstances and all times."*

Of the *necessity* for this interference, in our own country and at the present day, I entertain no doubt. Fully admitting the force of much that Mr. Baines has written, —admiring "his genuine English spirit," his energy, and his eloquence,—agreeing with him that Education is not only "far more extensive than it has been in any former period of our history," but that it is advancing at a much greater rate than heretofore,—attaching the highest possible value to every expression of a people's beneficence,— regarding the continuance of voluntary effort as essential to freedom of education,—prizing the agency it creates and sustains far above all price,—and much more disposed to wonder at what it has accomplished, than at what it has failed to perform,—I yet cannot, and *dare* not conceal my conviction that, both in amount and in quality, the education of the people of this country falls vastly short of what it ought to be, and that the continuance of such a state of things is utterly inconsistent with the safety, honour, or welfare of this great empire. Did the whole question turn on the position and prospects of British Schools alone, much as I value them, highly as I estimate the zeal and liberality displayed in their support, disposed as I naturally must be to take the most favourable view of their condition and character, I should still be obliged to confess that any impartial examination of them *as a whole*, would clearly demonstrate, so far as demonstration is possible, the utter inadequacy of the Voluntary Principle to educate the country.

But when the question involved is really nothing short of overtaking and subduing the ignorance and crime which rages like a pestilence among the untaught masses of our crowded towns, and the equally untaught inhabitants of our

* Dr. Vaughan. British Quarterly, VIII. 495, 6.

villages, the responsibility of opposing any measure at all calculated to accomplish the object is in my view *fearful.*

In forming an estimate of the numbers who need to be thus instructed, and of the money which must be raised to accomplish it, I will put aside altogether the estimates of the Government Inspectors on the one hand, and of Mr. Baines on the other; and I will simply refer to a document addressed to the churches of the congregational order in the county of Lancashire, by the Congregational Board of Education, and published in the Christian Witness, for the month of March, 1846, just twelve months ago. It is signed by order and in behalf of the Board, by Samuel Morley, chairman, and Robert Ainslie, secretary. As these two gentlemen are among the most active opponents of the Minutes of Council, no testimony can be more impartial. The article is long, and as the number which contains it may be obtained of the booksellers for a few pence, it is only necessary to give a brief extract :—

" The Board will now lay before you some facts which it has collected, and respectfully offer a few suggestions; and it is hoped that when they are seriously reflected upon, some great practical result will follow for the benefit of the county.

" The population of Lancashire in 1841 was 1,667,054, being an increase within the ten preceding years of 167,054, and at the same ratio of increase the present amount (December, 1845) is 1,742,226. The county is divided into seven hundreds, and the following table forms a summary of the whole.

SUMMARY OF LANCASHIRE.

Hundreds.	Children under 15.			Proportion for Day-school.			Gross Population.	No. of Ministers.	No. of Chapels.
	Boys.	Girls.	Total.	Boys.	Girls.	Total.			
Lonsdale, Nor.	5,024	4,774	9,798	3,350	2,183	5,533	26,747	1	1
Lonsdale, Sou.	6,211	4,433	10,644	4,141	2,956	7,097	34,760	1	1
Amounderness	16,913	16,894	33,807	11,276	11,263	22,539	93,033	6	7
Blackburn ..	37,965	37,555	75,520	25,310	25,037	50,347	193,832	11	13
Leyland......	10,640	10,302	20,942	7,094	6,868	13,962	54,299	4	4
Salford	138,468	140,673	279,141	92,313	93,783	186,096	764,654	38	48
West Derby ..	88,558	87,813	176,371	59,040	58,543	117,583	499,729	16	22
	303,779	302,444	606,223	202,524	200,633	403,157	1,667,054	77	96

"The preceding table has been compiled with great care.
The list of churches and ministers has been revised by the list
published in the Congregational Almanac for 1846, and has
been arranged according to the localities of the ministers in the
six hundreds of the county.

The tables of the Manchester Statistical Society are then
given at length, followed by a summary of the Gaol re-
turns for the County, and extracts from the Registrar
General's Report. This state of things it is added, cannot be suffered to exist.

" The disclosure of such facts is painful; but if they were uni-
versally known among the intelligent and religious portion of the
population, they would very soon be facts no longer. The property and Christian principle of Lancashire, with the intelligence
and skill of the leading persons in every town of the county,
would very soon, by God's blessing, bring about a different state
of things. There is abounding liberality in the county, and
abounding wealth. From the property-tax return, printed by the
House of Commons, in May, 1844, it appears that the annual
value of the *real property* assessed under schedule A in the
county amounted to the large sum of £7,105,248. 10s. 4½d., and
this is, of course, independent of all kinds of personal property.
" If all the children of the county that ought to be receiving
daily education were in humble life, the number being 403,157,
the cost of their education would be £302,368 annually; and
if each child paid twopence per week, they would pay for their
education annually £174, 701. 6s., leaving £127,666 to be provided by the friends of education.
" If we deduct one-third, or 134,385, as children that would
not attend even superior British schools, then provision would
be required for 268,772. The cost of their education would be
£201,579 annually, and, at twopence per head per week, they
would contribute £116,477. 17s. annually, leaving £85,102 to
be raised annually for county education. A voluntary offering
of threepence in the pound annually on the sum of £7,105,248
(being the annual value of the real property of the county)
would raise £89,648. 18s., a sum adequate to the purpose;

but in this calculation we suppose all schoolhouses to be built and kept in repair from some other funds."

Now on this document I have only *one* remark to make, —and it is this. If the education of the people of Lancashire is to be deferred until " threepence in the pound" can be obtained " *annually,*" as " *a voluntary offering*" on the sum of £7,105,248, the annual value of the real property of the county, it will in my opinion clearly be deferred to a day far too distant to affect the interests of the present generation.

It is no secret, that, in the year 1843, during the heat of the conflict respecting the Factories Education Bill, I published a pamphlet entitled, " The Bill or the Alternative,"—a letter to Sir James Graham. In that pamphlet, among other things, the following suggestions occur, which I quote chiefly for the purpose of showing that I am not now adopting any new views for the purpose of meeting a supposed emergency :—

1. " That, subject to the approval by the Committee of Council of plans and estimates, and subject, also, to a report by an inspector that such school was needed, and would probably be frequented by a sufficient number of children, two-thirds of the money required should be advanced by the Government, whether such application was made through the National Society, by Church of England schools not connected with that institution, through the British and Foreign School Society, by the Wesleyan Education Committee, by Unitarians, or by Roman Catholics.

2. " That, provided such schools were reported by the inspector to be efficiently conducted, one-half of the annual expense of such school, after deducting the payments of the children, should be provided out of the consolidated fund.

3. " That all such schools should be inspected by inspectors appointed by Government; but that to avoid the apprehensions and jealousies which have hitherto been excited by such inspection, the inspectors, while servants of the Crown, and indepen-

dent of the schools they examined, should be parties *having the confidence* of the educational or religious bodies whose schools they were to visit and report upon, and that the existence of this confidence should be ascertained prior to their appointment, by friendly correspondence with such bodies."

It was further added :

" Normal schools might be established and aided on similar principles, and perhaps some method might be devised for securing to decayed schoolmasters a suitable provision in their declining years. The absence of any such resource, it is notorious, is a greater hinderance to the continuance of efficient men in the employment of teaching, than even the miserable stipends they receive by way of what is miscalled remuneration."

Did it become me, I observed, to *argue* in defence of continuing and extending the various grants already made by Parliament in aid of voluntary effort, it would be impossible to omit observing, that

" England is the only country in Europe whose inhabitants are willing to meet, by voluntary subscription, to almost any extent, the efforts of the Government, in educating the poor ; that the constitution of no other state practically admits of that free and voluntary union of all ranks in well-doing, which makes the monarch and the merchant, the noble and the peasant, co-workers together for good ; and,—since nothing binds men together like benevolence—since nothing leads so naturally and surely to the discovery of mutual worth, as the co-operation of various ranks, in any great disinterested effort of charity,— England is the only country of the Old World in which it is possible for the Government, in every town and village, to attach itself by the strongest of all bonds, to the very classes with whom all political power ultimately rests."

Now, having published these views openly in 1843, the pamphlet in which they were embodied having had a large sale, and having subsequently seen no reason to change the opinions there expressed, need it excite surprise that, in April, 1847, I should feel inclined to pause and ponder, before I can yield assent to Mr. Baines's statement, that " the measure resolved upon by the Committee of Council," embracing, as it does, with slight modifications, every one of the foregoing suggestions, should have been " *designed* to conciliate the Church, without giving palpable ground of offence to Dissenters ;" should have been " *constructed* to give a great immediate advantage to the Church, and yet to open the way for the endowment of the ministers of every creed ;" that its " *one pervading principle* " is, " hostility to voluntary religion and voluntary education, and its certain tendency to bring all education and all religion under State pay ?"*

I know it may be said that other, and more perilous elements have been introduced into the Minutes,—that it is not so much the continuance or enlargement of grants in aid of school buildings, the inspection of schools, the payment of salaries, or the provision for pensions that is to be dreaded, as the enormous amount of patronage, arising both to the Government and the Clergy, out of the selection and support of paid monitors and pupil teachers, connected as this is with subsequent exhibitions to Normal Schools, and offers of employment in the public service.

I have been most anxious to give to all these points the most serious and candid attention. I have read the " Minutes " again and again, aided by all the light that can be thrown upon them by acute and able opponents. I have endeavoured to examine the whole question, with fairness and impartiality. And, having done so, I feel that no man has a right to blame me, if I have arrived at conclusions widely differing from his own.

Perhaps I cannot better explain the views I entertain in relation to the measure generally, than by plainly and

* Baines's Alarm to the Nation, p. 6.

decidedly stating my belief—without of course pledging myself to every matter of detail—

I. That the assistance thus offered to schools, will, if generally accepted, be productive of the greatest possible benefits to the community, tending to the immediate improvement of elementary education, and facilitating all subsequent endeavours to secure a continued supply of well-qualified instructors.

II. That English liberty will in no degree whatever be endangered, by the payments proposed to be made from public funds to schoolmasters, monitors, or pupil teachers, so long as such payments are checked and controlled by local committees.

III. That the provision made under the Minutes, for the selection, examination, and subsequent support of monitors, pupil teachers, and candidates for Normal schools, is just and equal, in no degree favouring the Established Church, or providing for her exclusive benefit.

IV. That there is nothing in the scheme at all bearing out the assertion, that it is either intended or adapted to facilitate the payment of ministers of all religious denominations.

V. That viewed fairly, and without prejudice, the plan proposed by no means excludes the most rigid and conscientious advocate of the Voluntary Principle in religion, from consistently sharing in its benefits.

VI. That the tendency of the whole measure, unless perversely thwarted, will, even in the rural districts, *eventually* be found favourable, rather than otherwise, to the interests of Protestant Nonconformity.

VII. That the hearty co-operation of all classes of the community, in carrying out its provisions, will afford the best and only security we can have *against* the introduction of a thoroughly organised State System of Education.

VIII. That the objections raised to the *mode* of its introduction, and to the *expense* that will be incurred in its operation, involving as they do, the constitutional characte of the Committee of Council,—the powers with which it may be invested, and the amount of money that shall be entrusted to it by Parliament, can only be discussed with advantage when viewed apart from any particular scheme or plan proposed by that body for promoting education.

I shall endeavour to establish each point as simply and as briefly as I can:

I.

The assistance thus offered to Schools, will, if generally accepted, be productive of the greatest possible benefits to the community, tending to the immediate improvement of Elementary Education, and facilitating all subsequent endeavours to secure a continued supply of well-qualified instructors.

I am not aware that this has been disputed. Mr. Baines seems to admit it, when he speaks of " great advantages" being " confined to schools which receive Government Inspection." But whether he does so or not, I can assure him that the benefit can scarcely be over-estimated. Every argument against the Monitorial System as adopted by the two societies, resolves itself into this,—'The agents by and through whom so large a portion of the instruction is communicated are too young, ill taught, and unremunerated.' The force of this objection cannot be evaded. Instead of diminishing by time, it has of late years been greatly increased in consequence of the growing facilities which are now afforded, both in the manufacturing and agricultural districts, for the profitable employment of children. The field and the factory alike outbid the school. The miserable pittance that has hitherto been allotted, even in the best British and National Schools, to the payment of monitors, cannot retain the children when other occupations offer their rewards. The fact need not be concealed. Both in the manufacturing and in the rural districts, the *purely* Monitorial System is rapidly becoming an impossibility.

The British and Foreign School Society has not slumbered over these things. Year after year have its Inspectors reported to the Committee the silent but sure operation of these social changes on the schools, and as regularly have they urged upon the attention of their friends the necessity for enlarged pecuniary contributions to secure the payment of monitors, and the support of assistant teachers. What has been the reply? 'We are unable. Already the school costs fifty, seventy, or a hundred pounds a year. If this new source of expense be introduced, it will be abandoned.' Is it possible under such circumstances to do otherwise than *hail* a provision for meeting this great master difficulty, supposing only (which has yet to be shown) that such provision can be accepted with honour and with safety?

II.

English Liberty will in no degree whatever be endangered by the payments proposed to be made from public funds to Schoolmasters, Monitors, or Pupil Teachers, so long as such payments are checked and controlled by local Committees.

The arguments of Mr. Baines and his friends on this point seem to me to overlook altogether two things; *first*, the existence, in all cases, of local Committees or Trustees, *in whom is vested the sole power* of dismissing at any moment, the schoolmaster, the pupil teacher, or the paid monitor: and secondly, that the Inspector can exercise no influence or authority whatever, except by the desire, or with the concurrence of this same local governing body, *with whom in fact all real power ultimately rests.* The

Inspector, properly speaking, cannot appoint a single monitor,—cannot select a single pupil-teacher,—cannot effect the slightest change in the order, discipline, or management of the school. He is not even to pay the money voted by the Government to the parties who are to be the recipients. At each and every stage of the proceeding, the local board must be recognized, consulted, deferred to. To talk of Government Patronage, under such circumstances, corrupting constituencies, influencing elections, emasculating the English character, is, to my mind, I say it with all possible respect for my friendly opponents,—infinitely absurd. To state broadly, and this has frequently been done, that such a system "resembles that of France,"—that it "has been drawn from the French pattern,"—that the French Governmental System "indicates the fruits" which it may be expected to bring forth, is monstrous.

Mark the points of difference! In France all teachers are "appointed by the Minister of Public Instruction, and can be suspended, removed from place to place, or dismissed, according to ministerial pleasure." In England, (supposing the obnoxious "Minutes" to be in full operation) not one can be either appointed, suspended, removed, or dismissed. In France all *private schools* are established only "by license from the Minister," and "they can be shut up by a simple Ministerial order, which," we are told, "frequently happens." In the "Minutes," private schools are not even noticed. In France, we are assured, a schoolmaster "cannot entertain liberal opinions, express them, or vote in their support at elections, without exposure to complete ruin." In England, the Whig or Tory ministry that should dare to tamper for a moment with the conscientious convictions of any class of the community, would be at once hurled from its high position with just indignation and well-merited contempt. In France, it is said, "bursaries or scholarships, of which there are about

2,000, are generally disposed of by the Minister in favour of the children of electors, or the relatives and dependents of deputies of their party." In England, under the "Minutes," the Minister cannot in a single instance present or appoint. But it is needless to go on. The two systems may be advantageously *contrasted;* but they can never be compared. To pretend that the establishment of a despotism like that of France is *the "object"* of Lord John Russell's Government in 1847, is surely mere irony.

It is easy enough to say, as Mr. Baines does, that the acceptance of Government aid even in the erection of a school-room involves an admission of "the right and duty of the Government to support and *direct* the Education of the people;" that "schools which receive Government inspection," are "virtually under Government control;" that if this principle be admitted, "Education might as well be at once placed under the absolute management of the Executive, like the collection of the revenue;" but such unfounded assertions carry no conviction with them; they merely strike one as being very hasty and very dangerous conclusions. It is equally easy to talk of peril arising from the retention of "88,000 new employés," or from the country being occupied by "an army of Government functionaries;" but one's alarm wonderfully subsides on finding that 30,000 of them are to be boys of 13 or 14 years of age, receiving from a local committee two shillings a week each towards their support for the first year, three shillings for the second year, four shillings for the third, and five shillings for the fourth, while engaged as assistants in schools; that a second 30,000 are youths a little older, receiving towards their maintenance, from four to eight shillings a week while in training for pupil teachers; and that the remaining 28,000 are students, schoolmasters, or labourers, over very few of whom the Government can exercise any authority whatever. And one is very apt to suspect the danger anticipated to be altogether imaginary, on finding that even " builders, architects, joiners, masons, and other tradesmen and handicraftsmen, will, though employed by the local Committees, still come in some degree under the influence of the Government." Taking things for granted at this rate, well may it be concluded that " the measure will bring under the distinctly perceptible operation of Government influence 400,000 or 500,000 families. I confess my inability to yield assent to such expectations.

III.

The provision made under the " Minutes " for the Selection, Examination, and subsequent Support of Monitors, Pupil Teachers, and Candidates for Normal Schools, is just and equal, in no degree favouring the Established Church, or providing for her exclusive benefit.

This is a simple matter of fact which may be ascertained by any one who will take the trouble to peruse the " Minutes." Do not let me be mistaken here. I am not saying that the measure will *work* equally;—*that* depends on circumstances hereafter to be considered. I am simply maintaining, and I do so without fear of contradiction, that the arrangements made for the selection, examination, and subsequent support of monitors, pupil teachers, and candidates for Normal Schools, are, as between Churchmen and Dissenters, just and equal. In each case the local Committee originates the application; —in each, the Inspector examines and reports; in each the services of the Inspector may be declined at the pleasure of the local Committee; in each the remuneration afforded to assistants is the same; in each an equal proportion of pupil teachers is allowed; and since the payment of these parties is independent of the amount raised by local contributions, the advantage, if there is any, must be on the side of the poorer body. I do not know that these things are disputed; we may therefore pass on to more delicate ground.

IV.

There is nothing in the Scheme at all bearing out the assertion, that it is either intended or adapted to facilitate the payment of Ministers of all religious denominations.

Public worship and popular education are not identical, nor will all the reasoning in the world, however ingenious, ever make them so. The one relates to a matter which properly lies between man and God only; the other involves great social interests, the peace and good order of society. The one is largely worship; the other is simply instruction. For his irreligiousness man is responsible only to his Maker; for his ignorance, if it be voluntary, and for the social consequences that flow therefrom, he is justly responsible to his fellow-man. Education is not *exclusively* a religious thing. If in one respect it involves spiritual privilege, in another it as distinctly includes civil right. To possess it is a secular advantage: to be deprived of it is to be brought under a civil disability.

I fully admit that the Minutes of the Committee of Council *recognize* religious instruction. I scarcely see how they could do otherwise. It is very easy to talk and write about Secular, or as it is sometimes termed, Moral Education, as distinguished from Religious Education; but it is practically impossible to sever them, unless, as Dr. Arnold says, "people have the old superstitious notion of religion, either that it relates to rites and ceremonies, or to certain abstract and unpractical truths." An able writer in the Quarterly Review, supporting in the main Dr. Hook's plan, says,—"If the school does not teach *re ligion*, may it not teach *religiousness?*" I do not know

c

that I quite understand the distinction, unless by religion is meant theology, and by religiousness the cultivation of gentle and devout affections apart from religious dogmas. If that be the meaning of the writer, and I suppose it is, the difficulty remains untouched; for how can any man cultivate the devout affections either in the young or old, apart from the constant recognition of those great truths which are "the power of God unto salvation," and on which his own soul lives, if there be any life in it? Banish altogether from the school every thought of God, —studiously exclude or keep out of sight every reference to man's moral condition, to a future state of existence, to eternal hopes, or unuttered fears; speak, act, teach, both by precept and example, *as if there were no God*, and you will have, but then only, a place of purely secular instruction. You may supplement this, I grant, by religious instruction given at stated times by Ministers of different religious denominations, for those who may choose to avail themselves of it, and so far conscience may be satisfied.— But you will inevitably do two things,—you will teach by this sort of unhallowed separation between things secular and things spiritual, a wretched lesson of practical ungodliness to every child that comes under your roof; and you will deprive probably *two-thirds* of the youthful population of England, of the only opportunity they may have for becoming acquainted, at least in early life, with the noblest thoughts that ever stirred the mind of man, the only thoughts that can control the turbulence of the will, calm the restlessness of the intellect, or satisfy the hunger of the heart.*

---

* In this and one or two other places, I have adopted a paragraph or two from former pamphlets, simply on the principle that no one has a better right than myself to any service they can render.

"*Two-thirds*." "I hold in my hand one of the Report-papers which are furnished weekly by our Scripture Readers to the Clergymen of

I admit, therefore, fully, that the Minutes of the Committee of Council do, and I think necessarily, *recognize the fact* that, in some form or other, moral and religious truth ought to be communicated to the masses of the population. But in relation to Dissenters they do no more: I do not know that I am warranted in affirming that they go even so far as this. Perhaps it would be speaking more accurately to say, that in relation to schools *not* connected with the Church of England they simply recognize the fact that, in some form or other, moral and religious truth *is actually*, by the free choice of the people of England, communicated in schools supported by voluntary contributions; and recognizing this fact they simply

---

their respective parishes. Their object is to show the work done in the week, the ground gone over, the houses visited, the number of hours employed. The column containing the number of persons visited is sub-divided into four portions, headed with the letters C, D, R, and N; C standing for Churchman, D for Dissenter, R for Roman Catholic, and N for a person who belongs to no Church, and has no brotherhood with any Christian community. Now I take the visits made by one reader in five successive days, and I give you the result as I have it in figures before me. On the first day, he visited families containing one hundred and fifty individuals; and of these, *one hundred* had no home in the Christian Church, no preference for any mode of Christian worship. On the second day, the proportion of these persons was yet larger, *seventy* being their complement to nineteen who owned a relation to one body of Christians or another. On the third day, by far the best, it is just half and half. On the fourth, for thirteen Church people and fourteen Dissenters, we have *sixty-two* with the black letter N annexed; and the numbers on the fifth day are almost exactly the same. Hear it, and ponder it, I pray you—in the metropolis of Christian England, out of five hundred and fifty persons, visited and talked with in succession, *three hundred and sixty*, or *two-thirds* very nearly, had no such connexion with the Church as to be assignable to any one religious body. Outcasts, we must surely call them, from the Christian family."—Rev. J. H. GURNEY.

Is it fair or right, in such a state of society, to treat Popular Education as if it were a question altogether between Churchmen and Dissenters?

require, that "the Managers shall certify of monitors and pupil teachers that *they are satisfied* with the state of their religious knowledge," or, as it is rather unfortunately expressed in another place, "that they have been attentive to their religious duties." The requirement, that in Church of England Schools, the Inspector (he being specially appointed for that class of schools alone) shall examine in the Catechism and Liturgy, is simply the recognition of other great facts, the existence of which it is not very easy for any of us to dispute, viz., that a Church Establishment exists in England, and that Catechism and Liturgy form part of the course of instruction in its schools. To say that this gives a legislative sanction to the teaching of the Church Catechism is, I think, altogether a mistake. Surely the Church of England has not had to wait until now for legislative sanction to its Book of Common Prayer, or to any thing that it contains.

I maintain, therefore, that the "Minutes" leave the Church of England, as to her schools, just where she was before their promulgation. They do not compel the teaching of catechism in a single school *where it was not before taught;* they do not withdraw it from any establishment into which it had previously been introduced.

Still less can the Government be said *to pay for teaching religion* in other schools. If it did so, it would be bound on its own principle to ascertain that the given religion was taught. It ought to examine, if not in the Wesleyan catechism, or in Butler, at least in the Scriptures; and if the Inspector were not satisfied with the *nature* as well as the extent of the scriptural instruction, the payment of the monitor or the pupil teacher should be withheld. He *would* do so, if the State professed or intended to pay for the religious teaching. But the State does not intend it: *therefore* the Inspector regards this subject as in a totally different position from all other subjects, and *in this department alone* is he content with the certificate of the local managers, that *they* are satisfied. The State very properly never gives money without a *quid pro quo*. In relation to secular teaching the *quid* is inspection, the *quo* the money; in religious teaching there is no *quid*, because there is no *quo*. But it is said the Bishop of Exeter has publicly avowed his intention of making schoolmasters Ecclesiastics, by conferring Deacons' orders upon them. If it be so, I do not see that the State can interfere or withhold payment, so long as the duties of the school are satisfactorily fulfilled. The Bishop need not wait for these Minutes of Council in order to fulfil his intentions. He can act upon his resolution at once if he chooses; just as the Wesleyan Conference may, on the same principle, authorize all its schoolmasters to act as local preachers. Such an evil---for I regard it as such, by whomsoever sanctioned---will cure itself. The obligations of the school will be found incompatible with the performance of ministerial duty. The assertion, that the *mere fact* of the schoolmasters' exercising ministerial functions involves the principle of payment for such services, will scarcely be maintained, when it is recollected that, for many years past, persons in the employment of Government have regularly acted as dissenting ministers, preaching every Sunday, and administering sacraments. On this showing, Government have long since paid ministers of all denominations; but who is so extravagant or absurd as to maintain, that in so doing, any principle has been involved on the one side or conceded on the other?

I admit, however, fully, and feel strongly, that the probability of schoolmasters, whether Anglican, Romish, or Dissenting, being allowed directly or indirectly to exercise, *as a class*, clerical functions, is a strong argument against

the payment by the State of any portion of their salaries.*
If any words of mine were likely to have weight with the
Government, I should very strongly urge, on this, *and on
many other accounts,* a re-consideration of that clause in
the Minutes which warrants the payment, under certain
circumstances, of sums varying from £15 to £30 annually,
in aid of the salary of schoolmasters. It is by no means
clear, that this arrangement will permanently add anything
to the comfort or emolument of *good* teachers, while it will
open a door to abuses which I fear no vigilance can check,
nor any power remove.

Many advantages would arise from at least deferring its
operation for the present. It would afford time to observe
the intentions of parties, and to see how other arrangements are likely to work. The proceedings of the Committee of Council must, I think, be regarded, to a certain
extent, as experimental. Everybody looks with *hope,* if immediate expectation be impossible, to the arrival of a time,
when the distribution of funds in furtherance of popular
education shall be entrusted to Municipal or District
Boards, and the sums requisite be raised by local assess-
ment. Probably no one, except Mr. Baines, really antici-
pates that millions of money will, for any length of time,
be scattered over the land at the pleasure of the Committee
of Council; no one feels that this would be in accordance
with the spirit of our institutions. But fixed and permanent arrangements seem essential, before the State can
take upon itself the payment of any portion of the salaries

* It is possible, however, that I may have misunderstood the
"Minutes" in this particular, and that it *may* be the intention of the
Government absolutely to refuse aid in all cases where schoolmasters
exercise Ecclesiastical functions. Such a resolution would, I think, be
fair, and be found to promote the efficiency of the schools; for nothing
but mischief can arise from the blending of duties so distinct as those
of the minister and the schoolmaster.

of teachers; for should Parliament, after agreeing to this principle, think fit greatly to reduce, or even to refuse the grant for a single year, distress would be universal. I express this opinion with great reluctance, because it may seem to be an unkind act in reference to the teachers; but I am quite sure that it is otherwise. The question is not, what is it fitting a well-qualified instructor should receive, but how can it best be secured to him? Is it advisable for a Government, in the present unsettled state of educational affairs, to take *a perpetual charge* of this sort upon itself, and to do so under circumstances which will call forth, however unfairly, unceasing complaints of bribery or of favouritism? The *gratuities* for instructing pupil teachers and monitors, being simply payments for extra work done, are altogether unobjectionable; while the provision for pensions will come into operation so slowly, that no risk will be incurred.

V.

Viewed fairly, and without prejudice, the plan proposed by no means excludes the most rigid and conscientious advocate of " the Voluntary Principle" in religion, from consistently sharing in its benefits.

Those who assent to the line of reasoning I have adopted in answering the objection, (made as I think without due reflection,) that the Minutes of Council involve the principle of paying the ministers of all religious denominations, will scarcely need any additional argument to satisfy them that a consistent adherence to the Voluntary Principle in religion, by no means involves the necessity of rejecting Government aid in education. But since it is too much to suppose that those who have adopted a different view of the question will be so easily convinced of the unsoundness of the ground they have chosen to occupy, as to express their willingness to accept aid for Congregational schools, and as the stress of the argument on the inequality and practical injustice of the measure, rests on the supposed inability of the Dissenters to avail themselves of advantages offered alike to all, it may not be amiss to show that, even on the assumption (which, be it observed, many Dissenters utterly disclaim,) that it is impossible to draw any clear distinction between the support of ministers and schoolmasters, provided both teach religion,—I say, even on the assumption, groundless as it is, that no distinction available for the present purpose can be drawn between the Congregational church and the Congregational school,—still, I am prepared to maintain that Voluntaries, as such, may, without any sacrifice of principle, avail themselves of Government aid in the promotion of popular education.

And I do so on this ground. They are citizens as well as Christians. They hold, and truly, that their christianity does not compel them either to resign or to neglect the rights and duties of citizenship. I venture to add, neither does it compel them, in the fulfilment of any public duty, to act as Nonconformists, when they can, with equal if not greater advantage to the community, act as Englishmen.

Why, then, should they not, in this capacity—as philanthropic citizens, as patriotic Englishmen, (and no one, who knows them *thoroughly*, will dispute their claim to that honourable distinction) combine to promote the education of their poorer neighbours on *what they may regard* as sound principles,—principles which will enable them consistently to share in the bounty of the State? If, like Dr. Vaughan,—not less my honoured friend because he may differ from me,—they think that it would not be lawful for them to receive money from the State for any school, unless "the general instruction be kept distinct from the religious, and the former be thrown freely open to the community, without any direct or indirect imposition of the latter," let them by all means adopt such an arrangement. For reasons already assigned, I think the plan of the British and Foreign School Society "a more excellent way;" but any way is better than standing still; any plan is better than allowing multitudes to live and die in ignorance, because we cannot agree as to the precise principle on which they shall be instructed. Let it be borne in mind, that I am now dealing simply with the objection of "the Voluntary." This argument, I am quite aware, will be of no avail with those who, like Mr. Baines, deny the right of Government to touch the question at all. I leave *them*, for the present, in the hands of Dr. Vaughan, who has, I think, unanswerably disposed of the abstract question, when he maintains that "it is impossible to separate between the *interest* of a nation and its *character*," and that "to say a Government may consistently do its best to help a nation to grow rich, but that it must not be supposed to care a jot about the influence which this money-getting may have upon its habits of industry, its intelligence, or its tone of moral feeling, would be to make distinctions the weakness or which becomes manifest the moment they are stated." I am now dealing simply with the "Voluntary" objection, and it is in reply to *that*, as stated by Dr. Vaughan, that I am urging the possibility of acting, in this matter, as a citizen rather than as a Dissenter; and consequently of receiving, in the former character, a benefaction which might very properly be refused in the latter.

It can never be too frequently stated, that this is not a distinction without a difference. It is a distinction that is felt and acted upon by all classes. The apostle Paul recognized it when he claimed the privileges of a Roman. English Dissenters have acted upon it to a far greater extent when, as magistrates, they have been called upon to sign warrants for seizures in consequence of the non-payment of church-rates. As a Dissenter, opposed alike to

State and to Sectarian schools, I hold that the direction of popular education is the proper duty and inalienable right of the people themselves; that it ought not to be resigned to the Government, that it ought not to be yielded to the National Establishment, that it ought not to be laid at the feet of the ministers of religion, either of one, or of all denominations. So complex a work is, I think, best promoted by religious men acting as Christian citizens,— representing in their movements *principles* rather than *sects*, and treating the subject *nationally* rather than *ecclesiastically;* that is, with reference to the country rather than to parties—to towns rather than to churches—to districts rather than to congregations. But it would, I think, be a perversion of reasoning, to insist that, because I hold this view, I am precluded from accepting either the agency of the church, or the money of the State.

Here, then, is a field in which Dr. Vaughan, and those who think with him, may not only work consistently and earnestly, but, in perfect harmony with their principles as Dissenters, reap all the benefit that can be derived from the much-abused Minutes of Council. It is no slight recommendation of such a course, that, by its means, the establishment of schools becomes practicable in certain districts where it would be otherwise impossible to act efficiently, and the temptation to appoint unsuitable teachers, merely for the sake of securing persons of peculiar religious opinions, is to a great extent removed out of the way.

VI.

The tendency of the whole scheme, unless perversely thwarted, will, even in the rural districts, EVENTUALLY *be found favourable rather than otherwise, to the interests of Protestant Nonconformity.*

I am quite aware, after what has been said and written

on this subject, that the assertion I have now ventured to make, will be received at first with something like a smile of incredulity. We shall see, in a little time, if it deserves to be so treated.

I presume that the opponents of the Government measure are as fully acquainted with the actual condition of the rural districts, at the present moment, as I am. They will not dispute that, with few exceptions, they are now, educationally, under the absolute control and influence of the Clergy. Of late years, a school has been established in almost every parish, generally on the most exclusive principles, and always identified with the Establishment. From these schools, the children of Dissenters are commonly shut out, unless they submit to conditions that involve something like " religious apostasy." A remedy for this state of things has long been sought, and sought in vain. Now let it be remembered, that this sad but true picture of *things as they are,* in hundreds of English villages and hamlets, is *the result of an all but purely Voluntary system :* for on Mr. Baines's showing, it can scarcely be maintained that these schools have been called into existence as the result of Government grants; for he insists, (I do not,) that " the increase of schools from 1833 to 1846," (the period of grants for school buildings,) has "not" been "equal to the increase from 1818 to 1833," when no such aid was afforded. If this be true, and I am willing, in order to avoid unnecessary disputation, to take it for fact on Mr. Baines's authority, then it proves beyond question, that, whatever may have been the motive, and I am unwilling to attribute an unworthy one, the zeal, energy, and success of the Clergy in the establishment of schools, has been most extraordinary. The truth is, as we all know, that the nobility and gentry of England, the owners of the land, and the possessors of wealth and influence in the rural districts, are, almost to a man, devoted to the interests of the English Church. At the instance of the Anglican Priesthood, land and money have been freely furnished for school buildings; and under the same influence, little doubt can be entertained, whether the Government aid or not, that the schools will, for the most part, be liberally sustained.

Now what great and marvellous change will be wrought in these districts, by the operation of the Minutes of Council? The schools will be improved,—the course of education extended,—that which is now too often a dead thing, will stand some chance of becoming a living thing:—is this in itself an evil? Will an enlarged education render the dull clod-hoppers of the hamlet less likely to become Nonconformists? Is it possible that, *under any system of training*, the quickening of the intellect,—the development of the faculties,—the acquirement of knowledge,—the breaking up of that "gloomy monotony," which John Foster termed "Death without its dance," can be unfavourable to Dissent? I should be very sorry to make such an admission. If I did so, Mr. Baines would, I fear, accuse me of being a traitor to my principles. Fully admitting that the most unlimited dispersion of knowledge cannot, in itself, ensure the advancement of wisdom and virtue, I yet fully agree with the eminent writer just quoted, that "utter ignorance is the most effectual fortification to a vicious state of the mind; not only defeating the ultimate efficacy of the means for making men wiser and better, but standing in preliminary defiance to the very application."

But I shall be reminded of "the fearful amount of influence and patronage given to the Parochial Clergy."

Whether the influence in question be exercised by the *parochial* clergyman, or by the occupant of an episcopal chapel,—whether it be shared by the laity, or monopolized by the priest, is a matter with which I think Dissenters have little to do. They may very safely leave Churchmen to settle their own quarrels, and to appropriate their respective shares of patronage and power. The objection of the Dissenters lies to the exercise of the influence at all. But *what is this influence?* Why, first, it is that which will arise from the power of certifying, year by year, the moral and religious character of all candidates for the office of pupil-teacher, or stipendiary monitor, in National or Church of England schools; and next, that which will accrue from being called upon to ascertain (a very suitable precaution, by the way,) that youths training at the public expense for teachers, are not inmates of houses in which evil and vicious example is nightly counteracting the training and instruction of the day. What new and extraordinary power will this responsibility give to a parochial clergyman? The supervision required must be exercise by some one. Can it, in relation to Church schools, with any regard to official propriety, be placed in more suitable hands than in those of the clergyman? If the laity of the Church of England view the deposit with jealousy, let them, by all means, insist upon a change; but Dissenters can scarcely be interested in such a matter. The idea of this influence being used for political purposes, is absolutely chimerical. In the first place, the monitors and pupil-teachers will not generally be the children of electors; and if they should be so, the influence capable of being exercised in connection with such small benefits,* is as nothing compared to that which is now wielded by the landlord over the tenant, the "good customer" over the trader, the master over the servant. Why, the English Clergy will

---

* I say "small benefits," advisedly; for, taking into account all the risks of failure, the loss suffered by employing the only years during which skill in any handicraft can be attained, in the occupation of the school; the chance of being thrown upon the world at 18, without a trade, and the certainty, in relation to the majority, that, at the best, a bare maintenance can be secured, may well justify the term "small benefits."

laugh to scorn the idea of the additional " political and ecclesiastical influence " given by the patronage of two or three monitors or pupil-teachers in a National school, (for it can scarcely be more in a rural parish,) being of the slightest moment to them.

Another objection, which has much more weight, certainly deserves grave consideration. It is this,—that in parishes where only one school can be supported, no security is taken for the admission of all classes, without violation of the rights of conscience. A provision to this effect was made in the Factories Education Bill,* and its absence from the " Minutes " has led some to express an opinion that the present measure is even *worse* than its ill-fated predecessor. But this is a hasty and unthinking conclusion. The Factories Education Bill proceeded altogether on a different principle. It was an attempt to establish a system of *combined* education on the basis, not of religious equality, but of religious toleration. It scarcely recognised voluntary efforts at all; the funds were to be provided out of local rates, and the schools to be governed by trustees elected according to law. But the present measure is of a totally different character. Its *principle* is to aid, *without controlling*, schools largely supported by voluntary contributions; and it is important for all parties that this principle should be preserved intact. If we once

---

* 66. " And be it enacted, That if the parent of any scholar shall notify to the master or trustees that he desires that such scholar may not be present at the periods when such catechism or portions of the liturgy are taught as aforesaid, it shall not be lawful for any person to compel such child to be present at such periods, nor to punish or otherwise molest such child for not being present; and it shall not be lawful for the trustees or master of the said school, or any other person, to give or permit to be given in the said school any religious instruction to such scholar, except the reading and teaching of the Holy Scriptures as hereinbefore appointed; and such child shall at the periods when such catechism or portions of the liturgy are taught as aforesaid be instructed in some other branches of knowledge taught in the school."

admit that, *as the price of aid*, Parliament may enforce new rules, or modify existing ones, voluntary subscriptions will soon come to an end, and liberty of Education, if not destroyed, will be seriously impaired. Having protected the Dissenter in Church of England Schools, the State would be bound in like manner to interfere for Roman Catholics and Jews in other schools; and, once beginning *to dictate*, I greatly fear it would before long control and absorb. I am inclined to think the Committee of Council have done the best they could, in stating that although "their Lordships have not by any of their Minutes attempted to enforce, they are nevertheless desirous to promote by their sanction and encouragement, such arrangements in Church of England schools as may provide for the admission of the children of persons not members of the Church of England, without any requirements inconsistent with the rights of conscience." And again, "If it should be found, that in any parish a Church of England school alone exists, that this school is aided by the Government, and that there are communicants of dissenting congregations too poor to provide for the education of their children, and who cannot conscientiously permit them to attend a school in which instruction in the Catechism and Liturgy is required from all the scholars; it would become their Lordships to inquire, whether the managers of the school feel themselves under the obligation of duty to enforce this condition. Such a result would be to be regretted, and it is believed would be rare; but if it existed, it would become the Government to deliberate in what way education could be provided for the children of religious parents, who conscientiously objected to permit their children to be taught the Catechism and Liturgy of the Church." *

---

* "The School in its Relations to the State, the Church, and the Congregation"—an admirable pamphlet, of a somewhat official character.

And of how little value after all are *any restrictions*, when forced upon distant and unwilling administrators! How easily are they evaded, how capable of being used for purposes of vexation and annoyance! Did the Dissenters regard the provision referred to as an important concession when it appeared in the Factories Education Bill? Not at all. They ridiculed it,—they rejected it,— they denounced it as "a mockery, a delusion, and a snare."

I do not wonder at this. Practically, such arrangements are little worth: they are not even shadows of better things to come. In such circumstances no effectual protection can be given, short of that which is afforded by a rival school. The difficulty which is found in sustaining such establishments, arises from the impossibility of inducing educated men—persons capable of instructing the children of farmers and tradesmen—to remain in villages without a large salary; *this* is the real hindrance both to religious liberty, and to the spread of Nonconformist principles.

And this brings me to the point at which, I think, the operations of the Minutes will *ultimately* be found favourable to the interests of Nonconformity. Supposing, as Mr. Baines imagines,—and again I take his calculations without at all adopting them as my own,— that in a few years annual grants will be made to 30,000 pupil teachers, and 30,000 paid monitors, what will be the inevitable result? Something like this:—In five years after the scheme shall have come into full operation, 30,000 youths of 17 years of age, and 30,000 more who must be at least 18 years old, will be cast upon the educational market; 3,000 he estimates may be transferred to normal schools, accommodation at present being provided for about 1100; a few hundreds (I scarcely see how it can be more) may be employed in the public service, and the remainder, 56,000, will be thrown upon the world, to obtain their livelihood as they best may.

Regarding, as I do, Mr. Baines's estimate of the number of persons that will be thus trained as most extravagant; for it by no means follows that because a school of 50 *may* have 2 pupil teachers, that therefore a school of 500 *must* have 20; I still think it inevitable that a very large number of intelligent, educated, and enterprising youths will, about the time referred to, be necessarily loose upon society, without the knowledge of any handicraft, estranged by their habits and training from the occupations of the vulgar, and ill fitted to bear up against the disappointed hopes to which a large number must be inevitably doomed. The effect, like that of other great social changes, will, in the first instance, be exceedingly painful to thousands; that the evil will ultimately right itself, and be productive of great and permanent benefit, I do not for a moment doubt. It will change altogether the status of elementary teachers. It will rapidly elevate the standard of admission into normal schools. It will give a more intellectual character to the instruction of the poor. It will displace many indolent and inefficient persons, and prove a sharp thorn in the side of more. It will *create a new class* in society, a class hitherto unknown in this country; persons who will unite an enlarged education with very lowly birth and connections, refinement with deep poverty. The benefit will not be unmixed with evil and danger. Many will be irreligious; many will be indolent and undisciplined; many will be ambitious and discontented. Still I see no other way in which the desired end can be attained; and since many more may reasonably be expected, under the Divine blessing on their instruction, to grow up faithful in the performance of duty, skilful in the government of the young, patient, firm, apt to teach, and eminently fitted for their work, I cannot but think that, on the whole, the advantages will greatly preponderate, and the Government and the country be fully remunerated for the labour that must be bestowed, and the expense that must be incurred.

But the particular feature of the change to which I wish to direct attention is this: *it will open the way for the easy and early establishment of schools by the Dissenters in every parish where ten families can be found.* The youths in question, wandering like poor scholars of the olden time, from home in quest of employment, competent to teach, and well skilled not only in elementary matters, but in the rudiments of algebra, and in the practice of land-surveying and levelling, will eagerly embrace any offer that may be made to them to commence a school in which the emolument arising from the instruction of the children of the farmers or tradesmen shall compensate for the admission of a limited number of the children of the labourers free of cost. A school thus commenced by a well-qualified teacher, will soon gather round it elements of strength and permanence; a committee of management will, in due time, follow; and there is then nothing to hinder its admission to a share in all the advantages of its more favoured rival. In this way, if in no other, I am satisfied the "Minutes" will work well for Dissenters. If the Bishops and Clergy have (which I for one do not believe) "*contrived*" these "Minutes" for the sake of exalting the Church at the expense of the Dissenters, they have not, I think, acted with their usual discretion. Instead of putting new checks upon the activity of their opponents, they have only afforded additional security for their liberty and liveliness.

VII.

The hearty co-operation of all classes of the community in carrying out the present measure, will afford THE BEST AND ONLY SECURITY *we can have* AGAINST *the introduction of a thoroughly organized State system of Inspection.*

Here the question arises, and it is a most important one, Is Mr. Baines correct or not in identifying the Minutes of Council with the designs of the Central Educationists? I think he is not. Those designs as avowed, defended, and plainly expressed, are in direct opposition to the present scheme. "Government," *say they*, "should enlighten and teach," not "yield to the prejudices and follies of a people who are to be taught." "Not in the hands of THE PEOPLE should be either the training or selection of public teachers; it is a task to which *Government alone* is competent." "For improvements to be generally and simultaneously adopted, they must be *enforced*, and this *by the State.*" "It is *just* to use compulsion *on the principles professed and acted on by all shades of German governments;* but it may not be expedient."

Now *test* the Minutes of Council by these statements, and observe the contrast. The Government does not *teach* anything at all. It has no power to select or to dismiss a single teacher. It does not even *attempt* to enforce a solitary improvement. It *disowns* all compulsion, and *rejects* without reserve all the principles professed and acted on by German governments. And yet Mr. Baines has brought himself to believe,—for I am sure he would not state it if he did not believe it,—that under the operation of the Minutes, "fifteen thousand schoolmasters will be placed in a state of absolute dependence on the Government of the day;" "babes" will become "venal;" "the very boy a parasite;" while "schoolmasters and pupil teachers," reduced to "servile bondage," will become "nearly as dependent on the Inspectors *as a slave in the United States is on his master.*"

Well may it be asked *how*,—by what unlooked for means, are these terrible anticipations to be realized? The *reply* is, by bribery and corruption; the *implication* that Englishmen of all classes are so venal that Government has only to offer a pecuniary inducement, and they are one and all ready to sell themselves, body and soul, to the State. I do not believe it. I think better of my countrymen. If they see the matter as I do they will *gladly* accept the bounty of the Government; they will *regard it as a duty* to co-operate with their Rulers in promoting the education of the poor. If they view the whole question in the light that Mr. Baines does, the same high principle that has enabled *him*,—however erroneously, as I think,— to lay aside every personal and party feeling, to forget old attachments and long-formed connexions, and to fulfil what he has deemed to be a great public duty, will sustain *them* in suffering, if needs be, for their conscientious convictions. Under such a condition of things, I do not believe that any Government could " lure away Dissenting schoolmasters,"—"lure away their scholars,"—"lure their School Committees to desert their principles," or "lure their subscribers to give up their subscriptions."

But that which I am most anxious to impress upon the friends of freedom, is this, that these Minutes, instead of promoting, afford the best and only security *against* the introduction of a thoroughly organized State system of education. They are the Alternative. I say so, because I regard it as a thing fixed and settled, with the concurrence of all political parties in the House of Commons, and in harmony with the proceedings of Parliament for the last fourteen years, that, (whatever Dissenters may say or think,) in some form or other, the Government of the country *will* promote the education of the poorer classes. *That* being settled, the only question remaining for consideration is, whether they shall do so *as co-operators* with the people, aiding voluntary subscribers, and leaving all substantial power with them; or whether, setting aside all existing arrangements, they shall adopt, by bill, a great parochial system, administered to some extent by local boards, but largely controlled by central Government power.

Supposing the latter course to be adopted, one of two things must, in the present state of public opinion, happen. Either the system adopted must be practically worked by the Church of England, the local influence, in the rural districts especially, falling, almost as a matter of course, into the hands of the Clergy; or, the State, stepping in as the protector of the liberties of Nonconformists, must, for that end, assume powers, the possession of which might, before many years have passed away, prove fatal to liberty of education. That is the alternative.

A liberal and patriotic Government, foreseeing dangers so real and imminent, has wisely adopted a course by which they may be avoided,—has resolved to secure freedom of education, by refraining from all direct interference with it, —and, aiding those only who are willing to aid themselves, has cast upon the people a large share of the responsibility, the expense, and the toil of securing their own rights and liberties. That for so doing Nonconformists will, at the coming elections, oppose or neglect them, is a supposition which my respect for that body will not allow me for a moment to entertain.

The view I have taken of the tendency of the "Minutes" to check any great centralizing movement, finds strong confirmation in the course adopted by the advocates of Continental Systems. In the first instance, the entire body, through the press, declaimed against the "Minutes," as falling far short of the just expectations of the country. The outcry of the Dissenters against them, on the score of their centralizing tendency, has converted most of these opponents into friends. But the Morning Chronicle, the steady and consistent advocate of State Education,—the untiring enemy of " the Societies,"—bowing to the Dissenters on the right hand and on the left, still holds on its way, complaining not of the *extent,* but of the *limitations* of State interference. It would dispense at once alike with voluntary subscriptions and voluntary management. Disdaining to distinguish between unprincipled subserviency to the managers of voluntary schools, and friendly sympathy with their labours; it denounces, as unsound and mischievous, the arrangement (essential in any case where voluntary subscriptions are mainly relied upon,) by which the Inspectors, while deriving all their authority from the Committee of Council, are appointed " with concurrence of parties." And, strange to say, unthinking friends of freedom of education are to be found ready to join in this absurd crusade, for the destruction of one of the most valuable checks we have against mischievous interference.

Perhaps I shall not find a better opportunity than the present, for stating my conviction, that the dangers of inspection *will be greatly lessened* by the operation of these Minutes. They will be so, because they supply *means* for effecting the improvements desired by the State. The unfortunate misunderstanding which, in the first instance, took place between the Government and the British and Foreign School Society, on the question of inspection, arose out of the anxiety of the Inspector to effect improvements which, however good in themselves, could not, on account of the expense involved, be accomplished through voluntary agency alone; and since no provision had then been made for meeting this difficulty, it followed, of course, that the schools, tested by a new and costly standard, were found defective, and foundations were laid for the construction of an argument against voluntary effort, and in favour of State education. This was *a practical injustice;* and hence arose the necessity for securing a greater harmony of feeling between the Society and the inspector. When these Minutes have taken full effect, the inspector will have a right to expect results in accordance with the assistance they supply.

VIII.

The objections made to the MODE *in which the Government measure has been introduced, and to the* EXPENSE *which may be incurred in its operation, involving as they do the constitutional character of the Committee of Council —the powers with which it may be invested, and the amount of money that shall be entrusted to it by Parliament, can only be discussed with advantage when viewed apart from any particular scheme or plan proposed by that body for promoting Education.*

The past history of the controversy abundantly illustrates the propriety of such a course. What can be more melancholy than to find, on the one hand a great political party, including men of the highest character, voting in 1839, resolutions condemnatory of the Order in Council, by which the very Committee on Education was appointed, which they are now approving and sustaining,—except it be to observe that the parties now in opposition were then as zealously "*hailing* the recommendations of the Privy Council referred to," and *praying* the House "to *extend further aid* from time to time, in accordance with the principle so recommended by the Privy Council;* Mr. Baines himself outstripping his coadjutors, and rebuking the Wesleyans for not supporting Government in language like this:—" If these objections succeed in obstructing this Government plan, the effect will be to obstruct all aid whatever to the education of the people. . . . . Do these men think that Government has no duties to perform ? Is every attempt to instruct the people to be clamoured down

* Petition of the Protestant Dissenters of the Three Denominations.

by bigotry?" Is it surprising;—I ask it with deep sadness,—that men who are unaccustomed to allow for the inconsistencies of human nature, reading and pondering these things, should express their conviction, as they do, that Churchmen and Dissenters are alike hypocrites, caring nothing either for the constitution or the people, but regarding simply their own miserable party interests? But this is the inevitable consequence of identifying great constitutional principles with the movements of either Whig or Tory partisans.

But *this*, Mr. Baines will indignantly exclaim, is no question of mere party interests. It is a great National Controversy. The liberties of Englishmen are at stake. A "monstrous violation of the constitution" is being perpetrated. Henceforward we are slaves. "If the people of England should be lulled asleep by the opiate bribes offered to them, and should permit their statesmen to accomplish these deeds of consummate state-craft, they will soon awake to the discovery that they are tied down, like Gulliver in the island of Lilliput, with ten thousand scarcely perceptible but sufficiently binding cords."

All this is certainly very startling, and, if true, very alarming. But let us take courage. Viewed in this aspect it ceases altogether to be a Dissenting question; Churchmen are as much interested in it as we are; and unless we come to the conclusion,—a very unreasonable one,—that all persons except ourselves are either too ignorant to comprehend, or too careless to value freedom, manliness, and all the great elements of the English character, we may rest assured that these "Minutes" in all their bearings will receive the most minute and searching scrutiny.

I cannot believe that the Parliament of England, the Aristocracy, the Church, the Free Church of Scotland, the Wesleyans, all more or less pledged to the Committee of Council, are either insensible to the value of liberty, or disposed to slumber when an enemy is at hand. My obstinacy may be unpardonable, but I really cannot bring myself to believe that darkness rests upon the dwellings of all these Egyptians, and that light is found only in our own little Goshen. Without, therefore, giving any opinion as to the constitutional character of the Committee of Council; at once admitting that its proceedings are open to objection from the very circumstances which render its existence necessary,—the temporary and transition character of educational movements; firmly believing that some form of municipal organization will ultimately be resorted to;—I am content to leave this branch of the controversy untouched, being fully assured that a free press, a powerful people, and a reformed Parliament, afford abundant security against any permanent violation of the British Constitution, or any enormous waste of public money.

I can now only refer very briefly to an incidental objection which has been taken in the course of the controversy, but which does not naturally range under any of the heads I have laid down. It is this: that there is no more need to provide bounties for the production of schoolmasters, than of blacksmiths or butchers. If this be true, all Normal schools, though supported entirely by voluntary subscription, are needless, and if needless, mischievous. The labors of all good men, for the last thirty years, in training schoolmasters, have, on this showing, been vain; our pleading has been vain, and your giving vain also. But this is not the fact. The qualities required in a schoolmaster are somewhat different from those that may adorn the most estimable blacksmith or butcher in the kingdom. " What is it we demand of the schoolmaster?—the devotion, the absolute and exclusive devotion, of the best of his years to a most important public service. We demand knowledge of various kinds, which he must not only possess, but be able to communicate to others; intelligence which shall be able to call forth the kindred intelligence of children in every stage of torpor, or languor, or obtuseness; a sagacious, an almost prophetic discernment of character and of capacity; a spirit which can not only bear with rude undisciplined dispositions, but with dispositions which have been, and still are, vitiated—rendered peevish, sullen, or passionate, by fond and injudicious, or by harsh and brutal parents; a skill which has to correct in a few school hours the perpetual mischief done in an ill-regulated home; temper which has often to endure the unreasonable complaints, the caprices, and the violence of the parents; discretion, which may sometimes have to contend with the officious interference of kind but foolish and conceited managers; firmness which will punish when necessary, but gentleness which will keep punishment down to its most temperate exercise; exemplary moral character, decency of dress, demeanour, unimpeachable integrity in money concerns; aptitude to discern the value of, and modesty to admit with gratefulness all real improvements in the art and science of teaching; self-respect, with proper deference to his superiors in station and in education.

" What do we entrust to the schoolmaster?—At least some part of the religion of our people; very much surely of their moral habits, their providence, their economy—their cheerfulness and content, their conscientious industry, their enjoyments, their amusements; their mental energies—in some degree their health; their attachment to the laws and institutions of their country; their independence of thought as Englishmen; their respect for social distinctions; their acquiescence in the difference of ranks and stations; their deference for legitimate authority; their dread of anarchy; their aversion to licentiousness; their peace, their happiness. What do we entrust to the schoolmaster?—We are persuaded that we do not exaggerate when we say—the destinies of England; the permanence of our constitution; the safety of the throne; the security of all our wealth, strength, and grandeur—our future welfare, glory, national existence. And to this schoolmaster we offer the pittance of a day-labourer—something below the gains of a prosperous artisan—something far below that of our domestic servants; this after having cultivated his mind, raised him to a level with, perhaps to conscious superiority over, many whom he sees basking in opulence—and with lucrative, improving, easy situations soliciting him on every side, vying for his service: and all this with not even a fixed or recognised position—even this miserable maintenance at best but precarious—still liable to be dispossessed of his poor pittance by the caprice of school managers, the failure of school funds, a fall in the wages of labour."*

Having thus disposed of the various objections which have met my eye in the numerous speeches and pamphlets of those who have attacked the measure, it only remains for me to say that no one rejoices more than I do at the growing jealousy which is felt in England of what is usually termed Centralization. I do not retract a single word that I have ever written in relation to this subject. I am only increasingly convinced of the necessity for incessant watchfulness over its stealthy approach. But jealousy has its limits, beyond which it becomes unjust suspicion, or unmanly fear. "There is danger in all enterprize, imperfection in all plans, abuse in all authority, corruption in all agency of man. But what Englishman counts this when the good preponderates?"

* Quarterly Review, CLVI., pp. 424, 5. The only apology I can make for the length of this extract, is its excellence.

It is because I cherish so great a jealousy of centralization in the public instruction of England, that I rejoice in the publication of Mr. Baines's letters. The information they contain as to the nature, working, and tendency of Continental Systems of Education will be found invaluable, when all controversies about the "Minutes" shall have passed away and been forgotten. Perhaps it was needful to his earnestness and his eloquence, that he should be fully possessed with the idea that the Government might safely leave the entire question untouched. I think time and further observation will lead to a change of opinion on this point; his *third* thoughts will, probably, be like his *first*, in harmony with those of his old friends the British and Foreign School Society.

In conclusion, I can only say, that my opinions, such as they are, have not been formed hastily, or committed to paper without long and anxious consideration. I have endeavoured to keep my mind open to the full and fair consideration of all the objections that have been raised to the Government measure. I attribute no motives to its opponents, save the purest and the best. I believe Lord John Russell, and his colleagues in the Ministry, to have been influenced by like simplicity of aim, and blamelessness of intention. Governments may be, as Lord Lansdowne says, "the worst of cultivators, the worst of manufacturers, the worst of traders," aye, and the worst of educators too; and yet it may be neither unlawful nor inexpedient for a free State to aid without directing, to help without controlling, the instruction of its poorer subjects. It punishes, —why should it not seek to prevent a necessity for punishment? It interferes to check the spread of poverty, one chief source of crime,—why should it not interfere to check the spread of ignorance, another and perhaps a greater source? It spends millions on prisons and penitentiaries;

why may it not, if needful, spend other millions in preventing the people from entering their polluting walls?

For myself—and I speak only as an individual—my mind is made up. If these Minutes, which I cannot doubt, should receive the sanction of Parliament, I shall do all I can, *consistently with duty*, to induce the friends of free and unsectarian education to accept the benefits they offer. For Dissenters to refuse taking any share of the Government bounty, unless they are prepared to make pecuniary sacrifices the extent of which they have not yet calculated, and the pressure of which will probably be found inconsistent with other obligations, is infatuation. It is practically handing over the education of the country either to the Church or to the State, or to both combined. It is to do their best to extinguish, *as a class*, Dissenting schoolmasters. It is to associate in the public mind, and to some extent in the public school, popular ignorance with Protestant Nonconformity, unjust and monstrous as such an association may be. It is to render our principles distasteful to the educated, and powerless with the masses. It is, in short, to commit a folly which may well be termed AN ACT OF SUICIDE.

I state these views decidedly, because I feel it due to those friends who have reposed any confidence in me as an individual, to be explicit as to the motives which have compelled me, with unfeigned regret, to appear in public as the advocate of a measure which they so decidedly condemn. But I do so, I hope, with modesty and self-distrust, sustained in no slight degree by the knowledge that many other friends, equally devoted and sincere, agree with me in the sentiments I have ventured to express. The fact that such wide differences of opinion exist among wise and good men on this as on every other subject, may well teach us all to exercise candour, humility, and forbearance in judging one another. The *sense of uncertainty* as to the probable effects of great measures on the welfare and happiness of our country, which is created in every rightly constituted mind by such diversity of sentiment, will deeply impress the thoughtful with a sense of the weakness and short-sightedness of man; and will lead the devout, under this painful sense of insufficiency, to fall back with joy and gratitude upon the assurance that "the Lord reigneth," and that "all things" shall "work together" to "fulfil the counsels" of a "Will," which with unwearying patience is ever occupied in educing good out of evil, order out of confusion, truth and love out of error, perversity, and strife. The Dissenters of England have not yet to learn that defeat is sometimes victory.

J. Rider, Printer, 14, Bartholomew Close, London.

www.ingramcontent.com/pod-product-compliance
Lightning Source LLC
Chambersburg PA
CBHW081304040426
42452CB00014B/2639